SCALES

and

CHORDS

II

A PROGRESSIVE APPROACH TO
LEARNING MAJOR AND MINOR SCALES

WENDY MURPHY FACHINI

Authorunit
Number and Address
877-826-5888
17130 Van Buren Blvd., Ste. 238, Riverside, CA 92504

Because of the dynamic nature of the Internet, any web addresses or links contained in this book may have changed since publication and may no longer be valid. The views expressed in this work are solely those of the author and do not necessarily reflect the views of the publisher, and the publisher hereby disclaims any responsibility for them.

ISBN: 978-1-958895-93-1 (Paperback Edition)
ISBN: 978-1-958895-94-8 (E-book Edition)

Printed in the United States.

Contents

This book is dedicated to all my piano students who have
tested the material in both of my books over the years and
also to my computer technology genius son Roger Fachini III.
I would also like to dedicate this book to my parents,
for whom I am forever grateful.

Introduction – How to Use This Book

The purpose of this book is to continue the progressive scale and chord exercises learned in book 1, while introducing new chord and scale patterns in major, natural minor, harmonic minor, melodic minor, and Chromatic Scales. "Scales and Chords II" is designed to be a supplement to any keyboard method of instruction and should be used after completion of the first Scales and Chords book. I have included appendices that include additional chord progressions, scale degree names, and triads on all the scale degrees for each major and minor scale.

Each level of instruction is rather involved. Beginning with Scale Pattern 1, the entire page of exercises is repeated in all major and minor scales. Every time a level is completed, the student begins the next level's exercises back in the key of C-Major. It should take at least twenty-four weeks to complete each level.

Preface

When I published the first Scales and Chords book in 2015, I did not think I would be publishing another book for a while. Scales and Chords II is the continuation of the progressive exercises that my teacher Roberta Buck wrote out for me as a young student. Up until now, none of my students had reached this level of instruction, so there was no testing pool for the material. As of January 2016, I have three students ready to enter Scales and Chords II, and their input will help shape this book for publication. It is my hope they will thrive on the thorough grounding of scales, chord progressions, and arpeggios found within. All musical structure is built around scales and chords, and they will leave my studio well prepared for advanced instruction.

The Circle of Fifths

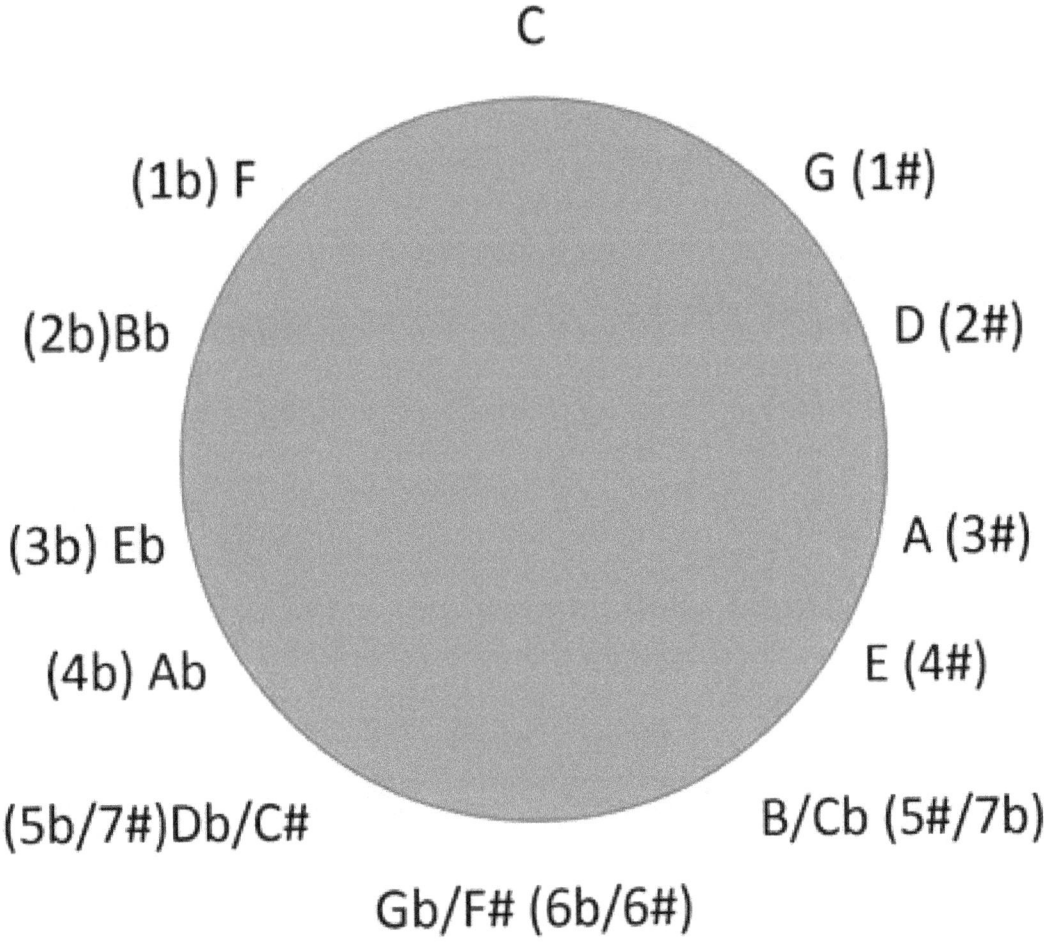

C

(1b) F   G (1#)

(2b)Bb   D (2#)

(3b) Eb   A (3#)

(4b) Ab   E (4#)

(5b/7#)Db/C#   B/Cb (5#/7b)

Gb/F# (6b/6#)

The circle of fifths is important because it shows the relationship of the keys to each other. C-Major at the top has no flats or sharps in its key signature. Going clockwise until C#, each key cumulatively adds a sharp to its signature in the following order: F#, C#, G#, D#, A#, E#, B#. Going counterclockwise from C-Major to Cb, each key cumulatively adds a fl at to its signature in the following order: Bb, Eb, Ab, Db, Gb, Cb, Fb.

Scales Level 1

1. All major and harmonic minor scales, four octaves hands together, ascending and descending.

C-G-D-A-E-B-F-Bb-Eb-Ab-Db-Gb

a-e-b-f#-c#-g#-eb-bb-f-c-g-d

2. Broken chord arpeggios and inversions, ascending and descending, in the fol owing patterns 1-4, hands together:

3. Do the following pattern hands together for each key studied:

4. Chords and Inversions: I – IV- I – V- I

5. Chromatic Scale, four octaves ascending and descending, hands together. Begin on the tonic note.

Scales Level 2

1. All major and harmonic minor scales, two octaves, hands together in the fol owing pattern:

Ascend legato/Descend staccato

Ascend staccato/Descend legato

C-G-D-A-E-B-F-Bb-Eb-Ab-Db-Gb

a-e-b-f#-c#-g#-eb-bb-f-c-g-d

2. Broken chord arpeggios and inversions, ascending and descending, in the fol owing patterns 5 and 6:

3. Run triads hand over hand up the scale. Make up a rhythm.

If major scale: I – ii – iii – IV – V – vi – vii dim – I

If harmonic minor scale: I – ii dim – iii+ – iv – V – VI – vii dim – i

4. Chord progression

If major: I – vi – ii – IV – V – V7 – I

If harmonic minor: i – VI – ii dim- iv – V – V7 – i

5. Chromatic Scale hands together, four octaves, staccato beginning on tonic of key.

Scales Level 3

1. a. All major scales, four octaves ascending and descending, hands together.

C-G-D-A-E-B-F-Bb-Eb-Ab-Db-Gb

b. All minor scales in natural, harmonic, and melodic form, two octaves ascending and descending, hands together. All minor scales have the same key signature as their relative major scale. A natural minor scale adds nothing. A harmonic minor scale raises the seventh note of the scale half step. A melodic minor scale raises the sixth and seventh notes of the scale, half step ascending, and is a natural minor scale descending.

a-e-b-f#-C#-g#-eb-bb-f-c-g-d

Natural   Harmonic   Melodic

2. Dominant seventh (V7) chords and inversions, hands alone.

3. Broken chord arpeggios and inversions, ascending and descending, in the fol owing patterns 7 and 8:

4. Chromatic Scale, hands together, two octaves contrary motion.

Scales Level 4

1. All major and harmonic minor scales, four octaves hands together.

Ascending pp<ff / Descending ff >pp.

C-G-D-A-E-B-F-Bb-Eb-Ab-Db-Gb

a-e-b-f#-c#-g#-eb-bb-f-c-g-d

2. Two octave arpeggios, hands together.

   a. Chord in LH/2 octave arpeggio in RH

   b. Two octave arpeggio in LH/Chord in RH.

3. Diminished seventh chord and inversions.

4. Sixth chords and inversions.

5. Chord progression and inversions

   If major scale: **I – vi – ii – V7 – I**
   If minor scale: **I – VI – ii dim. – V7 – i**

6. Chromatic Scales, two octaves hands together in parallel thirds, with LH beginning on the tonic of the scale and RH a third above.

Scales Level 5

1. All major and harmonic scales, two octaves hands together.

    Ascend scale/Descend arpeggio

    Ascend arpeggio/Descend scale

C-G-D-A-E-B-F-Bb-Eb-Ab-Db-Gb

a-e-b-f#-c#-g#-eb-bb-f-c-g-d

2. Run arpeggios through the chords in the scale. LH replaces RH.

3. Run the following tonic (I) chord progression hands alone.

M, m, dim, M, Aug, 6th, M7th, Mm7th, mm7th, dim7th, M

4. Chord progressions

    I – I dim – V7 – I
    I – V dim – V7 – I

5. Chromatic Scales, two octaves hands together in parallel 6ths, with LH beginning on the tonic and RH a sixth above.

Scales Level 6

1. All major and harmonic minor scales, two octaves hands together as follows:

   Ascend scale/Descend chromatic
   Ascend chromatic/Descend scale

C-G-D-A-E-B-F-Bb-Eb-Ab-Db-Gb

a-e-b-f#-c#-g#-eb-bb-f-c-g-d

2. Broken chord arpeggios in patterns 1, 2, 3, and 4.

3. Arpeggiate the chords through the scale. Hands together, two octaves, ascending and descending.

4. Chord Progression

   If major key: I – iii –vi – IV – vii dim – ii –V7 – I
   If minor key: I – iii+ – VI – iv – vii dim – ii dim – V7 – i

5. Chromatic Scale, hands together on tonic, as follows:

Scales Level 7

1. All major and harmonic minor scales, two octaves hands together, ascending and descending in the following pattern:

    First me – LH staccato/RH legato

    Second me – LH legato/RH staccato

C-G-D-A-E-B-F-Bb-Eb-Ab-Db-Gb

a-e-b-f#-c#-g#-eb-bb-f-c-g-d

2. Broken chord arpeggios in patterns 5, 6, 7, and 8, hands together.

3. Chord progression

I – I+ – I dim – vi – ii – IV – V7 – I

4. Chromatic Scale, three octaves contrary motion, hands together.

Scales Level 8

1. All major and harmonic minors in the following Grand Scale pattern: C-G-

D-A-E-B-F-Bb-Eb-Ab-Db-Gb

a-e-b-f#-c#-g#-eb-bb-f-c-g-d

2. Summary of broken chord arpeggios in books 1 and 2. All eight patterns hands together.

3. Chord progression

I – v minor – iii – vi – ii – V7 – I

4. Chromatic Scale in the Grand Scale pattern above.

Appendix I

Additional cadences and chord progressions:

I – vi – vi7 – ii7 – V7 – I

I – iii – vi7 – ii7 – V7 – I

I – vi – IV – V+ – V7 – I

I – ii7 – V7 – vi7 – IV – V7 – I

Appendix II

Scale Degree Names:

Major: I – ii – iii – IV – V – vi – vii dim – I

Minor: I – ii dim – iii+ – iv – V – VI – vii dim – i

First note = Tonic, tonal center, key name

Second note= Supertonic, a whole step above the tonic

Third note= Mediant, midway between tonic and dominant

Fourth note= Subdominant (5th) lower than the tonic

Fifth note= Dominant, fifth above the tonic

Sixth note= Submediant, midway between tonic and subdominant

Seventh note= Leading Tone, leads melodically half step up to the tonic.

Appendix III

Additional Broken chord Arpeggio patterns: 9, 10, 11, and 12.